The ABCs of Sailing

Written by Allison Hynes
illustrated by: Badrusoleh

For Ariel and Ben

A is for Anchor, to hold the boat in place

B is for Buoy, to sail around in a race

C is for Captain,
the brave leader of the crew

D is for Dock,
where you return your boat to

E is for Electronics,
to turn on all the lights

F is for Flag, flying high as a kite

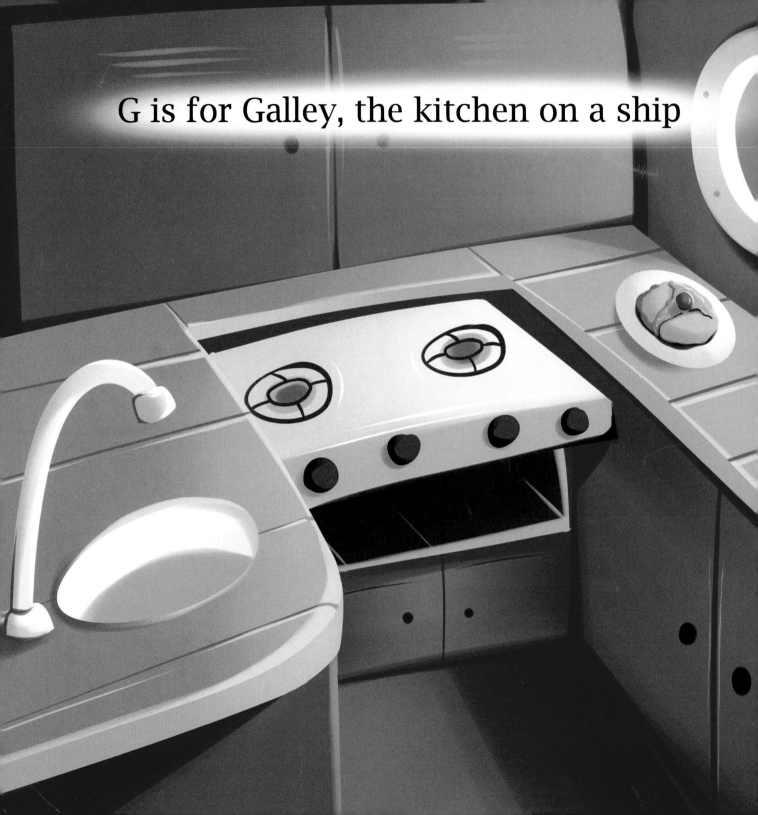

G is for Galley, the kitchen on a ship

H is for Helm,
steer the wheel with a tight grip

I is for Island, a sunny destination at sea

K is for Keel, the fin that steadies the boat

L is for Life preserver, to keep you afloat

M is for Mast,
the tall spar holds up the sail

N is for Navigate,
chart your location without fail

O is for Ocean,
a large expanse of water with no land in sight

Q is for Quick,
pick up speed with no fear

R is for Rudder,
which helps the boat steer

S is for Spinnaker,
a large sail flown in a race

T is for Tack,
change direction upwind and pick up pace

U is for Underway,
you're out sailing in the sun

V is for Voyage, a long journey, what fun!

W is for Wind,
it propels the boat for your pleasure

X is for X marks the spot,
find the buried treasure

Y is for Yacht,
another name for your boat, yo ho ho!

Z is for Zig Zag, the path your boat takes when you tack, away we go!

Now that you know your sailboat from A to Z,
Grab your life preserver and
come sailing with me!

Made in the USA
Coppell, TX
05 August 2020

32604248R00019